Learn To Make Quilts with Flannel Fabric

Bobbie Matela, Managing Editor
Carol Wilson Mansfield, Art Director
Linda Causee, Editor
Meredith Montross, Associate Editor
Christina Wilson, Assistant Editor
Terea Mitchell, Illustrations
Graphic Solutions, Inc-chgo, Book Design

For a full-color catalog including books on quilting, write to:
American School of Needlework®
Consumer Division
1455 Linda Vista Drive
San Marcos, CA 92069

We have made every effort to ensure the accuracy and completeness of these instructions.
We cannot, however, be responsible for human error, typographical mistakes or variations in individual work.

©1997 by Terry Johnson-Huhta.
Published by American School of Needlework®, Inc; ASN Publishing, 1455 Linda Vista Drive, San Marcos, CA 92069

ISBN:0-88195-835-2   All rights reserved.   Printed in U.S.A.   1 2 3 4 5 6 7 8 9

A Word From the Author

The quilts featured in this book were designed and constructed by "Lofty Ladies of the Cloth." Our name came about because we were all employed at the "Quilt Loft" in Moscow, Idaho. We ladies are a tight-knit group who quilt together, scheme together and enjoy all life has to offer. We can often be seen scouting out quilt shops and quilt shows. Each year we spend a weekend retreat sewing, chatting and eating. We are a small off-shoot group of Palouse Patchers, whose book *Watercolor Log Cabin Quilts* was published by ASN in 1996. This latest book was written because we wanted to see how creative we could be using the new flannels with traditional quilt blocks.

The members of the "Lofty Ladies of the Cloth" are Claudia Anderson, Krista Bateman, Celia Boland, Rosanne Cosgrove, Jackie Greenwalt and me. This book would not have been possible without their talents and eagerness to try something new.

ACKNOWLEDGEMENTS

Thanks Bob, for encouraging me to try this book stuff again. Hugs and Kisses.

A special thanks to my "lofty" friends. They hold a special place in my heart.

And, I certainly cannot forget the great folks at ASN. They always publish a high quality book.

Terry Johnson-Huhta

Introduction

As babies of a different era, we first experienced the soft cuddly warmth of flannel in the diapers that mom used. This soft, durable fabric was perfect for soft bottoms and for the many launderings it would endure. It's unfortunate that today's children are diapered in scratchy, stiff paper. As we grew, the pajamas and nightgowns were made of pretty downy pastel flannels. What a delight on a cold winter's night to be attired in this warm, fluffy fabric.

Flannel has traditionally been used for sleepwear and it is an ideal fabric for work and casual clothing. Flannel is the ultimate for sheets. There is nothing more enjoyable than climbing into a freshly made bed with cozy flannel sheets. Or, how about the backing for a treasured crazy quilt that Grandma made. Flannel fabric seems to invoke numerous pleasant and happy memories for many of us.

The flannel quilts presented in this book use many traditional pieced and appliquéd blocks. These blocks are easy to construct using quick piecing techniques and fusible web to appliqué. The edges of the appliqués are secured using either a hand or machine Blanket Stitch.

With the introduction of the many new and varied flannel fabrics on the market, it is the perfect opportunity for quilters to try using them. Not only are the traditional plaids and soft pastels available, but many paisleys, calicos, large splashy florals and wonderful rich solids are available as well. Flannel fabric is also suitable for hand dyeing. The fabric readily grabs the dye. Many vibrant colors and hues can be achieved. If hand dyeing sounds interesting, there are numerous books that detail the steps.

The quilts in this book each use various techniques. The individual instructions give the yardages, special piecing and appliqué techniques used and any templates required.

Making a Flannel Quilt

What You Should Know About Flannel

Flannel is typically a 100% cotton woven fabric and it can be handled much the same way as good quality 100% cotton fabric. Here are some special considerations and techniques to use for flannel quilts.

• Pre-wash flannel as it tends to shrink a bit more than regular cotton. Wash the flannel in warm water with your regular laundry detergent and place in the dryer to fluff. Promptly remove it and press.

• Flannel fabric is a soft fabric to sew on and the stitches tend to sink into it. Be especially careful removing stitches as it is easy to snag or tear the fabric.

• The easy appliqué technique, Fusible Web Appliqué, used in the quilts in this book works beautifully with flannel fabric. Flannel gives the appliqué a soft look, there's minimal fraying and the Blanket Stitch gives a nice finished edge to the raw edges of the appliqué pieces.

• Quilting a flannel quilt is fun and easy when using our Chunky Stitch Quilting technique, page 7. There's no need to worry about getting tiny even stitches. Instead, use a long running stitch with pearl cotton or six strands of embroidery floss.

• When pressing, do so gently to avoid stretching the fabric and press on the wrong side. With flannels, because they are sometimes heavier, the seam intersections might lay flatter if they are pressed open, rather than to one side, to distribute the bulk.

• It is a good idea to clean and oil your sewing machine when working on flannel quilts since flannel creates more lint than regular cotton fabric.

• Use a ¼" seam allowance when sewing.

Fusible Web Appliqué

The appliqués in this book use a fusible web product such as Steam-a-Seam 2®, Wonder Under®, or Aleene's Fusible Web®. The manufacturers of each of these products give specific instructions on how to use them. For best results, follow the instructions on sample pieces of the flannel fabrics.

Hand Blanket Stitch

Pearl cotton in size #8 or #5 or two to three strands of embroidery floss are used for the hand Blanket Stitch. The stitch is usually worked from left to right. Hold the thread down with your thumb and make a downward stitch. Bring the needle up over the thread, **Fig 1**.

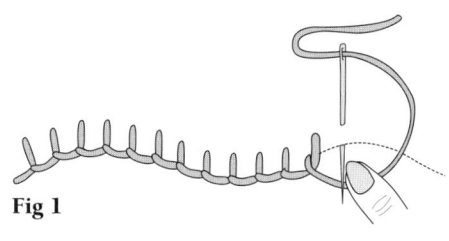
Fig 1

Machine Buttonhole or Blanket Stitch

Sewing machines with decorative stitches usually have a Buttonhole or Blanket-type stitch, **Fig 2**.

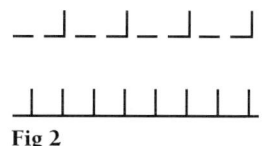
Fig 2

Topstitching thread or two strands of hand quilting thread are used. The bobbin thread is the same color as the top, but use regular machine sewing thread.

Use an embroidery sewing machine needle. It has a larger eye and the larger threads glide through it more easily.

Practice first on fabric scraps that are the same as your quilt project. To begin and end stitching, take a few stitches in place. Experiment with the stitch width and length until the stitch mimics a hand Blanket Stitch. Sew slowly, manipulating the stitches around curves and corners. With a little practice, the stitches will be hard to distinguish from the look of hand work.

Other Stitch Options

If your machine does not have the Blanket Stitch, perhaps it may have a Feather Stitch, **Fig 3**, or some other stitch that looks similar to hand embroidered stitches. A zigzag stitch can even be used, **Fig 4**.

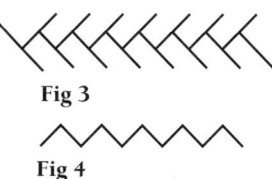
Fig 3

Fig 4

Adding Borders

Strips may need to be pieced to achieve the desired length. Piece the strips by sewing the ends diagonally, right sides together at right angles. Sew diagonally corner to corner. Trim ¼" from stitching and press open, **Fig 5**.

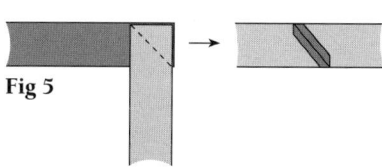
Fig 5

Straight Borders

Lay the quilt top out on a flat surface. Find the length of the quilt by measuring through the center of the quilt for Measurement A, **Fig 6**. *Note: Measuring through the center is more accurate than measuring along the edges. The quilt may have become stretched with all the seams and handling.*

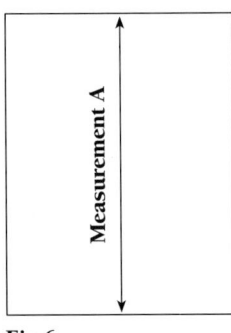

Fig 6

Cut two border strips the width needed and the length of Measurement A. Find the center of both the quilt and the border. Pin the border to the quilt matching the centers and both ends. Ease in any fullness. Sew, then press seams toward borders.

Lay the quilt out again and measure the width including the newly added borders for Measurement B, **Fig 7**. Find center edges of both the quilt and the border. Again, pin the borders to the quilt, matching centers and ends. Sew, then press seams toward border.

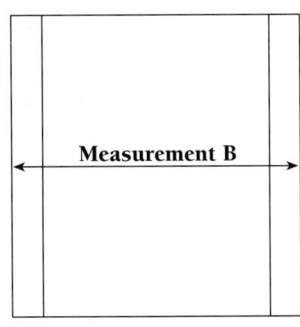

Fig 7

Repeat this process if you have decided to add more than one border.

Mitered Borders

Lay quilt top on a flat surface; measure to determine the length (A) and width (B). Write these two measurements down. Decide on the width you want your borders. If you want multiple borders, sew them together and treat them as one border.

Cut two border strips: the length of (A) plus two times the width of the finished border plus an additional 4". There will be a generous amount of overhang on each edge of the border. This is needed to miter the corners.

Find the center point of each side of the quilt top; place a pin at center to mark. Beginning on one side of quilt top, pin ¼" from each end. Repeat on opposite side.

Find center point of each border strip; place pin at center to mark. Measure out from center one-half the measurement of A; place a pin ¼" inside that measurement, **Fig 8**.

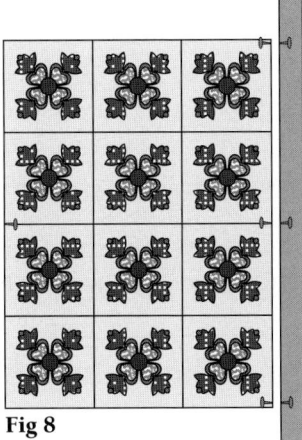

Fig 8

Pin border to quilt, matching pins. Begin sewing ¼" from end of quilt (at pin) and stop ¼" from opposite end. Repeat on other side of quilt.

Cut two border strips the length of B plus two times the width of finished border, plus and additional 4". Attach strips to top and bottom in same manner as for sides. You should have two tails extending from each corner of the quilt, **Fig 9**.

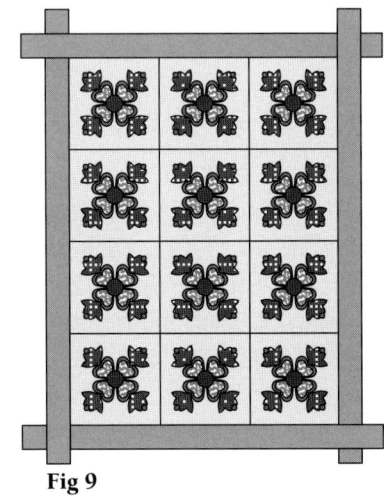

Fig 9

At the ironing board, fold top tails back onto lower tails to produce 45 degree angles, **Fig 10**; press. Sew seam in crease stopping ¼" from inside corner; trim tails leaving ¼" seam allowance, **Fig 11**.

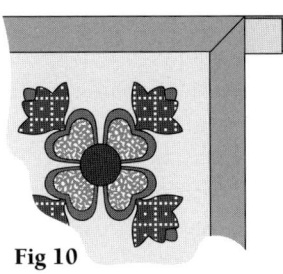

Fig 10

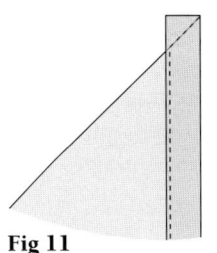

Fig 11

The Backing

Every quilt top needs a back on which to sandwich the batting. Choose something that complements your work and with fiber content of 100% cotton.

It may be necessary to piece the backing to make it large enough. To avoid a center seam in the backing, use three panels instead of two. The backing should measure 2" beyond on all four edges of the quilt top.

The Batting

Batting content, whether it be 100% polyester, all cotton or a blend of the two is a personal choice. If the quilt is to be hand quilted, a thinner batt is desirable. If a cotton batt is used, it will need to be quilted much closer than a bonded polyester batt. Read the manufacturer's instructions on the packaging. A recommendation is given as to how to treat the batt. Be sure to purchase a batt large enough to extend 2" to 3" beyond the quilt top on all sides. Some of the batting will need to be encased in the binding.

Layering and Basting

Quilts need to be basted together before doing any machine or hand quilting. If the quilt is to be commercially machine quilted, check with the quilter first as the basting step is usually not needed. Press backing carefully to remove all wrinkles. Place the backing on a large table if available or on the floor, right side down. Tape the edges to hold it firmly in place. Next, carefully spread out the batting on the top of the backing. Smooth out all wrinkles. **Hint:** *If the batting is allowed to rest over night, it will relax a little.* Place quilt on top of the batting, centering it over the backing and batting; smooth all wrinkles. Basting can be done using large running stitches, spaced about 3" to 4" apart. Safety pins (size #2) are also sometimes used. The safety pins are placed approximately a "fist's" width apart. You'll use a lot of them. Whichever method is used, start from the center and work toward the outside edges. **Hint:** *This is a great time to call a friend; this is a tedious job.*

Chunky Stitch Quilting

After the quilt layers have been secured, it is time to quilt. Most often the quilt is attached to some kind of frame to keep it tight while it is quilted. There are many books on the market that discuss hand quilting extensively. There are also hundreds of quilting patterns and stencils available. Check with your local fabric shop. After the quilt is quilted, DO NOT trim the batting and backing until after the binding is attached.

The quilts in this book use Chunky Stitch quilting. This technique is an extra large running stitch, about $\frac{1}{4}$" long and using #5 pearl cotton thread. This thread is available in a wide array of colors. Chunky Stitch quilting is charming when incorporated with the homey look of the flannel quilts. Any quilting design would be appropriate and an added bonus is that this stitch works up quickly!

Machine Quilting

The quilt may also be quilted on the machine using a walking foot or a free-motion foot. There are many excellent books available describing the techniques to successfully machine quilt. Also check in the yellow pages for professional machine quilters. They have large machines that do a wonderful job if quilting is not something you wish to try. Be sure to tell your machine quilter NOT to trim the batting and backing. Some of the batting and backing needs to extend into the binding.

The Binding

Measure the distance around the outside edge of the quilt and add 12". This is how long your binding will need to be. Divide this number by 42" (usable width of most fabrics). The resulting number will determine how many strips of fabric will need to be cut. Then multiply this number by the width of the unfinished binding. Typically this is $2\frac{1}{2}$" - 3".

Example:
Distance around quilt ... 368"
 divided by 42" = 8.76
 strips needed 9
 9 strips x $2\frac{1}{2}$"=22.50" of fabric
 or $\frac{3}{4}$ yd

Seam the ends of the binding together on the bias (See **Fig 5** on page 5.) Press binding strips in half lengthwise wrong sides together the entire length. DO NOT trim the batting and backing until after you have attached the binding. Some batting needs to be in the binding to add firmness to it. Attach the binding to the quilt using a $\frac{1}{4}$" seam allowance. Begin anywhere but in a corner, leaving a 6" tail for connecting—the center of the bottom is a good place. Continue sewing until you are $\frac{1}{4}$" from a corner. Fold binding strip so it forms a right angle with edge of quilt, **Fig 12**, then fold back down so raw edge is even with raw edge of quilt. Continue sewing, **Fig 13,** and repeat process at remaining corners.

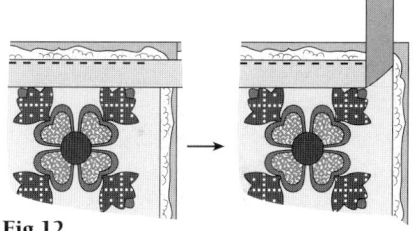

Fig 12

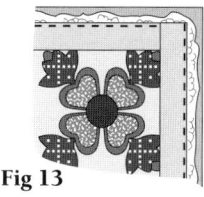

Fig 13

When completely attached, trim the backing and the batting slightly beyond the edge of the quilt. Fold binding toward back and hand stitch in place. Miter will form automatically at each corner.

Bias Binding

A 30" x 30" square of fabric will yield enough bias binding for Winter In Bloom, page 20, and a 20½" x 20½" square of fabric is enough for It Might As Well Be Spring, page 9.

Fold binding fabric in half on the diagonal and then in half again to form a triangle, **Fig 14**.

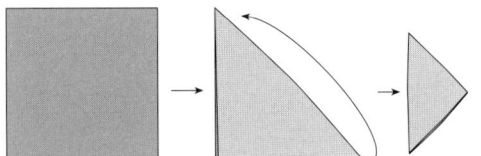

Fig 14

Cut double fold off and, leaving the fabric folded, use the newly cut straight edge as a guide; cut enough bias strips to equal the distance around the quilt plus 12", **Fig 15**.

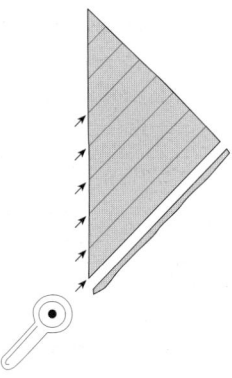

Fig 15

Sew strips end to end right sides together; press seams open, **Fig 16**. Gently press the long bias strip in half lengthwise wrong sides together.

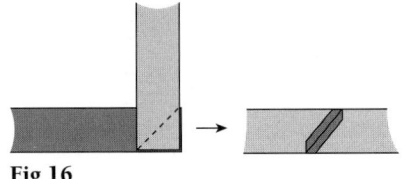

Fig 16

Line up raw edge of binding with edge of quilt top, **Fig 17**. Pin in place as you go to avoid stretching.

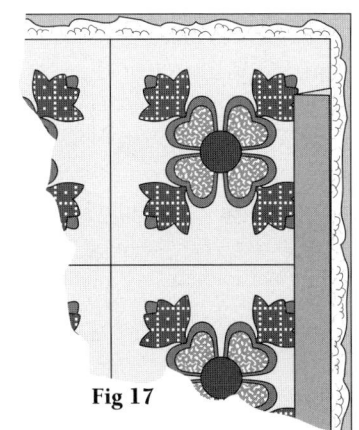

Fig 17

Beginning on the side (not a corner) of the quilt, leave a 6" tail and sew a ¼" wide seam allowance around the quilt to within 7" from the starting point.

Remove quilt from machine and cut the binding so that it overlaps the beginning by at least 5 ".

Pin each loose end of binding to quilt, pinning until the two ends meet, **Fig 18**. Sew binding ends together where pins meet. Finish sewing binding to quilt.

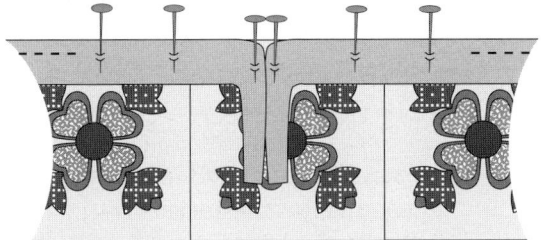

Fig 18

Trim batting and backing to at least ¼" from seam, being certain that binding will be full when turned.

If quilt top has scalloped edges, such as It Might as Well be Spring, page 9, clip all inside corners (can clip outer corners as well to help quilt lay flat). When clipping, be certain to clip no more than ¼".

Fold binding toward back and hand stitch in place.

Making a Label

The quilt is almost completed. A label will need to be made. Include who made it, the name, the date and any other interesting information. Be creative and use any technique. Cross stitch is beautiful, or indelible ink pens can be used to make lovely labels.

It Might As Well Be Spring
by Rosanne Grunlund Cosgrove

Quilt Layout

Shown in color on page 14

Approximate Size: 38" x 38"
Finished Block Size: 4½"

Let that special baby in your life feel the joy of spring and enjoy the look of these pretty pastel flowers all year 'round. This pretty pastel quilt looks like spring but keeps baby warm through those cold winter months. The design is easy enough for a beginner to tackle. It has just enough Blanket Stitch appliqué to make you wish you had more to do.

Materials and Supplies:

¼ yd of six different pastel flannel prints (blocks and prairie points)
¾ yd white or off-white flannel (background)
¼ yd solid pastel (second border)
1 yd striped pastel flannel (third border)
1¼ yds pastel flannel (backing)
⅝ yd solid pastel flannel (binding)
batting (at least 2" wider and longer all around than quilt top)
½ yd lightweight fusible webbing
#5 pastel pearl cotton
large embroidery needle

Pattern Pieces (page 12):
A Flower
B Flower Center

Cutting Requirements:
Note: *Strips are cut on the crosswise grain.*
one 2" x 44" strip from each of four different pastel flannel prints
four 2" x 44" strips, white flannel (cut two strips into 26 - 2" squares)
three 2" squares from each of six different pastel flannels
two 5" x 44" strips, white flannel (cut into twelve 5" squares)
eight 3" squares from each of six different pastel flannel prints
four 1¾" x 44" strips, white flannel (first border)
four 1¼" x 44" strips, solid pastel flannel (second border)
four 6" x 44" strips, striped pastel flannel (third border)
2"-wide bias strips, solid pastel (binding)

Instructions:

Block Assembly

1. Sew a 2"-wide pastel print strip lengthwise to each side of a white background strip; press seams away from background strip, **Fig 1**. Repeat with remaining two pastel print strips and one background strip.

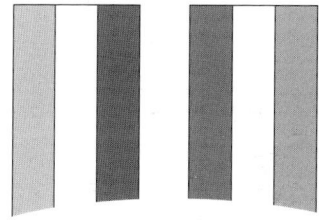

Fig 1

2. Cut thirteen 2"-wide units from each strip-pieced fabric from step 1, **Fig 2**.

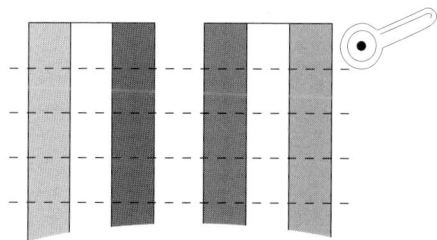

Fig 2

3. Sew a 2" white square to opposite sides of a 2" pastel square, **Fig 3**. Repeat for a total of thirteen units; press seams away from background strips.

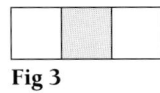
Fig 3

4. Take two units from step 2 and place on either side of a unit in step 3. Sew together to form a Nine-Patch Block, **Fig 4**; press seams to one side. Repeat for a total of thirteen Nine-Patch Blocks.

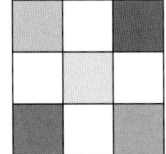
Fig 4

5. Trace twelve each of Flower A and Center B onto paper side of fusible webbing, **Fig 5**.

Fig 5

6. Cut outside the line of each Flower and Center, **Fig 6**.

Fig 6

7. Press each Flower and Center onto wrong side of a variety of pastel fabrics following manufacturer's directions on the fusible webbing.

8. Cut along drawn lines of Flowers and Centers; peel off paper backing.

9. Place Flowers and Centers in position on the 5" x 5" white background squares, **Fig 7**. Once these are in place, press according to the manufacturer's instructions.

Fig 7

10. Following the instructions on page 5, appliqué using Blanket Stitch around the Flower and Center in each block.

Quilt Assembly

1. Lay out the Nine-Patch and Appliqué Blocks in five rows of five blocks referring to layout. Sew blocks together in rows, then sew rows together.

2. Measure through the middle of the quilt from top to bottom and cut two 1¾"-wide white strips to that measurement. Pin these strips along sides of quilt and sew in place. Be careful not to stretch the fabric.

3. Measure again from side to side and cut the two remaining 1¾"-wide white strips to that measurement. Pin and sew in place.

4. Repeat steps 2 and 3 with the 1¼"-wide solid pastel strips for second border.

5. For Prairie Points, fold and press each 3" pastel square in half on the diagonal and then in half again, **Fig 8**. Place raw edge of eleven Prairie Points along each side of the quilt adjusting them so they are evenly spaced, **Fig 9**. Pin in place and machine baste ⅛" from the edge on all four sides.

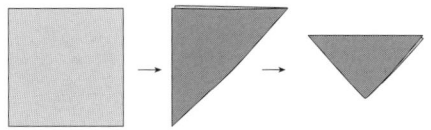
Fig 8

Fig 9

6. Refer to Mitered Borders, page 6, to attach the 6" striped pastel border.

Layering, Quilting and Binding

1. Using the Scallop Pattern on page 12 as a guide, draw the scalloped edge along outside edge of quilt top, **Fig 10**.

2. See pages 6 to 8 for layering and quilting. The photographed quilt was Chunky Stitch quilted using pearl cotton as follows: $1/4$" away from outside edge of each flower; $1/4$" inside edge of each Appliqué Block; diagonally through white squares of Nine-Patch Blocks; straight down center of first border and in a scallop pattern in the third border. Machine quilting was done in the first border.

3. After quilting is complete, machine baste about $1/8$" outside of scalloped line. (This is the edge of the quilt).

4. Attach binding referring to Bias Binding, page 8.

Fig 10

Scallop Pattern

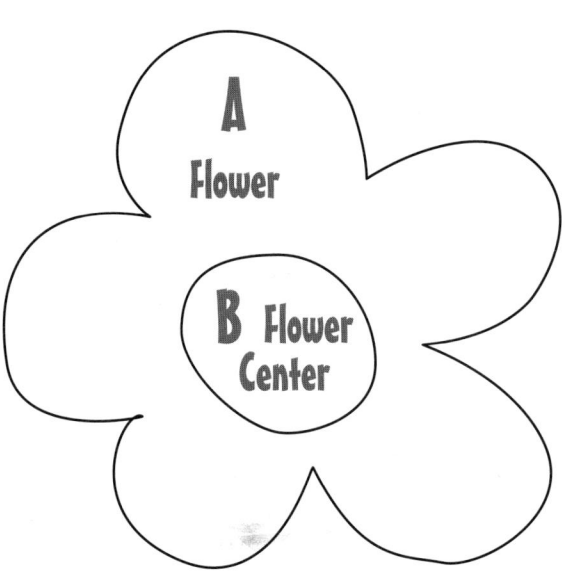

My Soft Flannel Rose

It Might As Well Be Spring

Winter in Bloom

A Twist of Tulipan

A Twist of Tulipan
by Claudia Zook Anderson

Quilt Layout

Shown in color photograph on page 16

Approximate Size: 60" x 76"

Tulipan is the Norwegian word for tulips and even though it may be cold outside, these tulips may help remind you that spring is just around the corner. The two panels of twisting tulips are appliquéd while the three panels of scrappy "braids" are pieced. The 1930's braid pattern uses an assortment of light and dark flannels. Add Blanket Stitching around the flowers, stems and leaves and Chunky Stitch Quilting in the wide border, then curl up in this cozy quilt and wait for spring!

Materials:

¾ yd burgundy flannel (tulips and inner border)
¼ yd assorted green flannel prints, (leaves/stems)
1⅔ yds tan flannel, background
⅛ yd 12-20 assorted lt flannels, braid panels
⅛ yd 12-20 assorted dark flannel prints, braid panels

Note: Fat quarters work great for these braid panels or an assortment of scraps that are at least 2½" x 7½".

2 yds green plaid flannel (outer border and binding)
4½ yds dk print flannel (backing)
2 yds 90"-wide lightweight batting
1 yd paper-backed fusible webbing
#5 pearl cotton or 3 strands of embroidery floss
large embroidery needle
template plastic or cardboard

Pattern Pieces (pages 18 and 19):
A, A Reversed
B Tulip
C Stem
D Leaf

Cutting Requirements:
70 - 2½" x 7½" strips, assorted lt and dk flannels (about 35 of each)
two 9" x 60" strips, tan flannel (cut lengthwise)
six 2"-wide strips, burgundy flannel (cut crosswise)
four 7½"-wide strips, green plaid (cut lengthwise)
five 2½"-wide strips, green plaid (cut lengthwise)

Instructions:

Making the Braid Panels

1. Trace patterns A and A Reversed onto template plastic or cardboard.

2. Layer several light 2½" x 7½" flannel strips with right sides up. Place template A even with end of strip, **Fig 1**. Butt up an acrylic ruler next to diagonal edge of template. Remove template and rotary cut along edge of ruler through all layers, **Fig 2**. Continue for all light flannel strips.

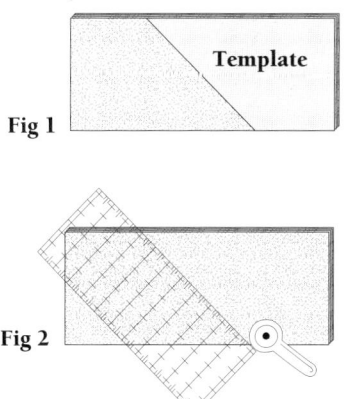

Fig 1

Fig 2

3. Repeat step 2 with remaining 2½" x 7½" dk flannel print strips and A Reversed template.

4. Sew a light A piece to a dark A reversed piece, **Fig 3**. Note position of pieces.

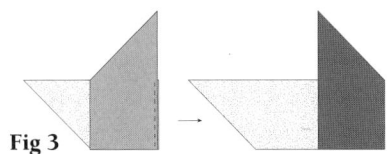
Fig 3

5. Sew a lt flannel A piece to lower edge of first and second pieces, **Fig 4**.

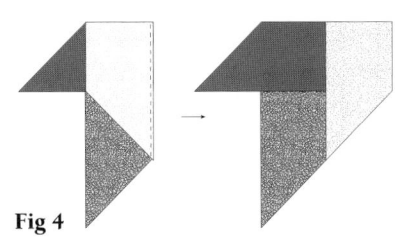
Fig 4

6. Add a dk flannel A reversed piece, **Fig 5**.

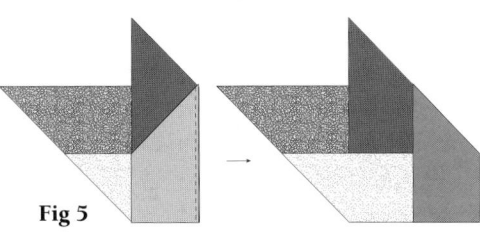
Fig 5

7. Continue in this alternating manner until braid panel is about 60" long, **Fig 6**.

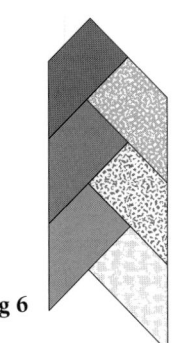
Fig 6

8. Repeat steps 4 to 7 for five more braid panels.

9. Place two braid panels on a flat surface, lining up center points; trim top and bottom edges, **Fig 7**. Measure strips and trim to 60".

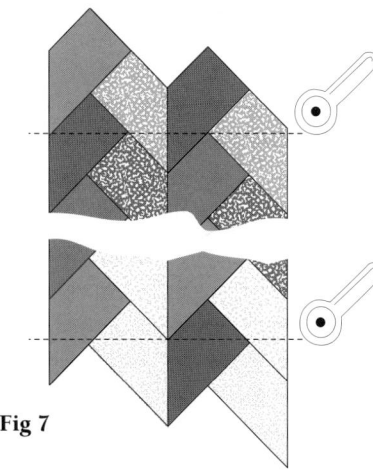
Fig 7

Tulip Panels

1. Prepare ten Tulips, ten Stems, and 50 Leaves using paper-backed fusible web referring to Fusible Web Appliqué, page 5.

2. Position Stems, Leaves and Tulips on the 9" x 60" tan strips, **Fig 8**, keeping the same distance from top and bottom and each side. Fuse in place following manufacturer's directions.

3. Blanket Stitch around Tulips, Leaves and Stems to complete panels.

Finishing

1. Sew braid and appliqué panels together referring to layout on page 17.

2. Add first border to quilt, sides first, then to top and bottom. Repeat for second border.

3. Refer to pages 6 to 8 to finish the quilt. The photographed quilt was machine quilted in the ditch on the Braid Panels and machine quilted ¼" from edges of Tulips, Stems and Leaves as well as stipple quilted loosely around the Tulips in the Appliqué panels. Chunky Stitch quilting using the Quilting Pattern on page 19 was done in the wide border.

Fig 8

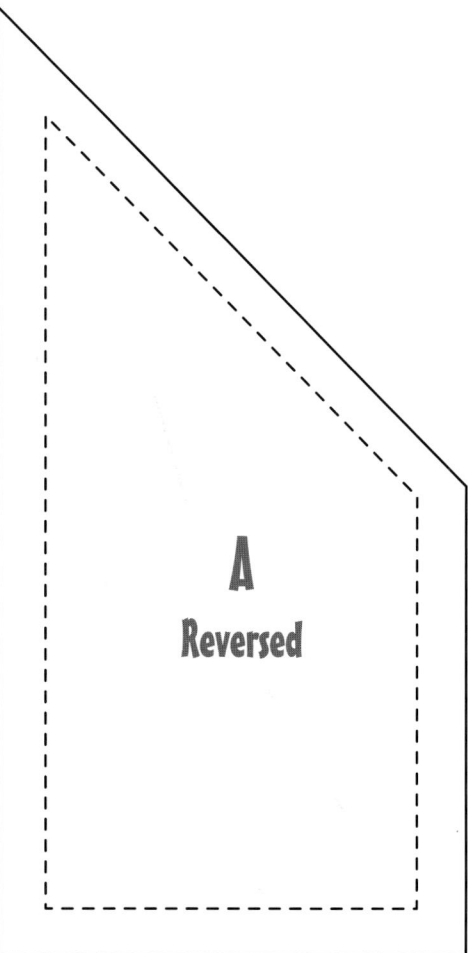
A Reversed

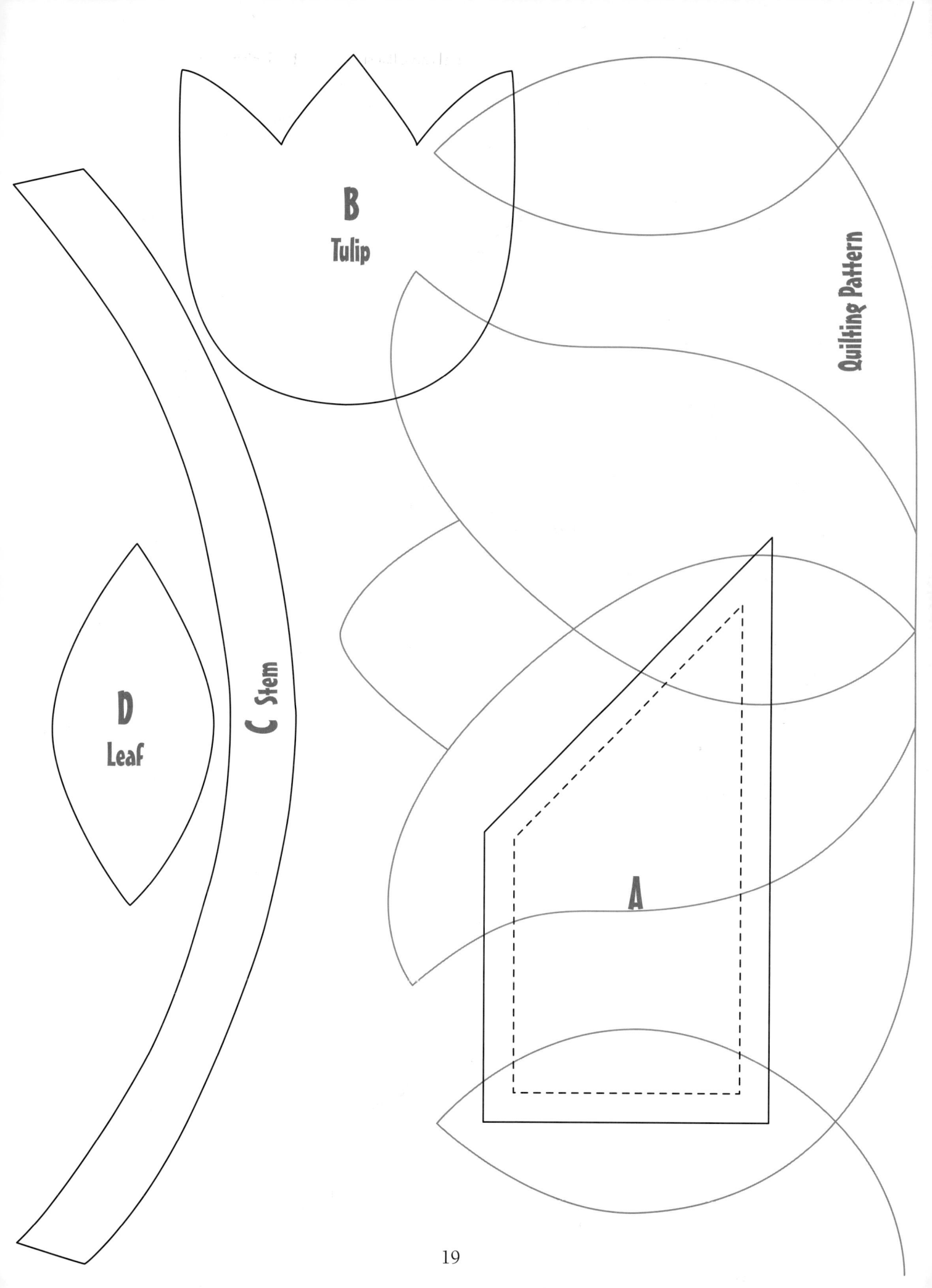

Winter in Bloom
by Rosanne Grunlund Cosgrove

Blanket Stitch 4½ x 4½

Quilt Layout *Shown in color photograph on page 15*

Approximate Quilt Size: 72" x 88"
Finished Log Cabin Block Size: 8¾"

This quilt will keep you warm in the winter while blooming all winter. This simple log cabin quilt is quick and easy to piece, leaving ample space to Blanket Stitch appliqué the folk art baskets and posies onto the background. Collect an assortment of plaid and printed flannels to make this wonderful, warm quilt.

Materials & Supplies:

3½ yds total of eight different dk flannels
3 yds solid or very subtle lt tan flannel
6 fat quarters, med to dk assorted flannel prints for Flowers, Baskets and Leaves. (Plaids make great baskets when set at a 45° angle)
¼ yd green flannel for stems
1 yd flannel for inside border and corner squares in border
2¼ yds dk print flannel for outside border
2½ yds lightweight fusible webbing
1¼ yds binding
5½ yds flannel for backing fabric
batting at (least 2" wider and longer all around than quilt top)
two spools of #5 black pearl cotton
large embroidery needles

Pattern Pieces (pages 23 to 25):
A1 Flower
A2 Flower
B1 Flower
B2 Flower
C Flower
D Tulip
E Large Leaf
F Large Leaf
G Bud
H Calyx
I Flower Center
J Basket
K Basket Handle

Cutting Requirements:
Cut 48 of each:
  1¾" x 1¾" squares, assorted dk flannels (center square 1)
  1¾" x 1¾" squares, assorted lt flannels (log 2)
  1¾" x 3" strips, assorted lt flannels (log 3)
  1¾" x 3" strips, assorted dk flannels (log 4)
  1¾" x 4¼" strips, assorted dk flannels (log 5)
  1¾" x 4¼" strips, assorted lt flannels (log 6)
  1¾" x 5½" strips, assorted lt flannels (log 7)
  1¾" x 5½" strips, assorted dk flannels (log 8)
  1¾" x 6¾" strips, assorted dk flannels (log 9)
  1¾" x 6¾" strips, assorted lt flannels, (log 10)
  1¾" x 8" strips, assorted lt flannels (log 11)
  1¾" x 8" strips, assorted dk flannels (log 12)

1¾" x 9¼" strips, assorted dk
   flannels (log 13)
Cut the following on the crosswise grain:
   four 8½" squares, lt tan flannel
   eight 2" strips, lt tan flannel
   eight 8½" strips, dk print flannel

Instructions:

Log Cabin Blocks

1. Sew a lt 1¾" square to dk 1¾" square, **Fig 1**; press seam to one side.

2. Referring to **Figs 2** to **12**, sew Log Cabin strips in numerical order. Press seams toward outside of block as you sew.

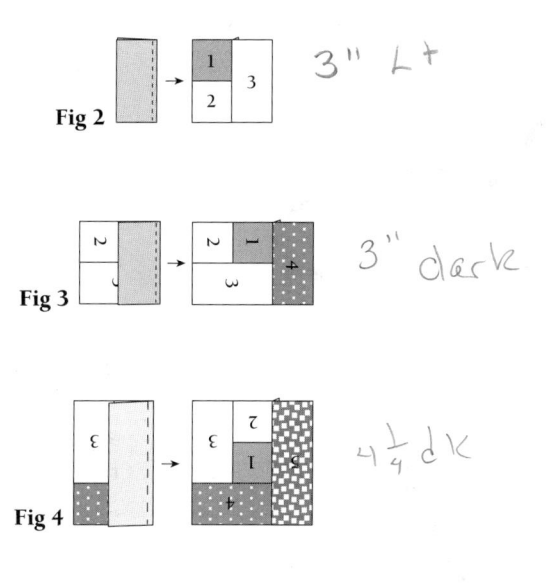

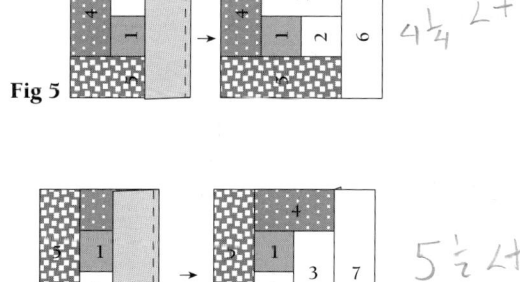

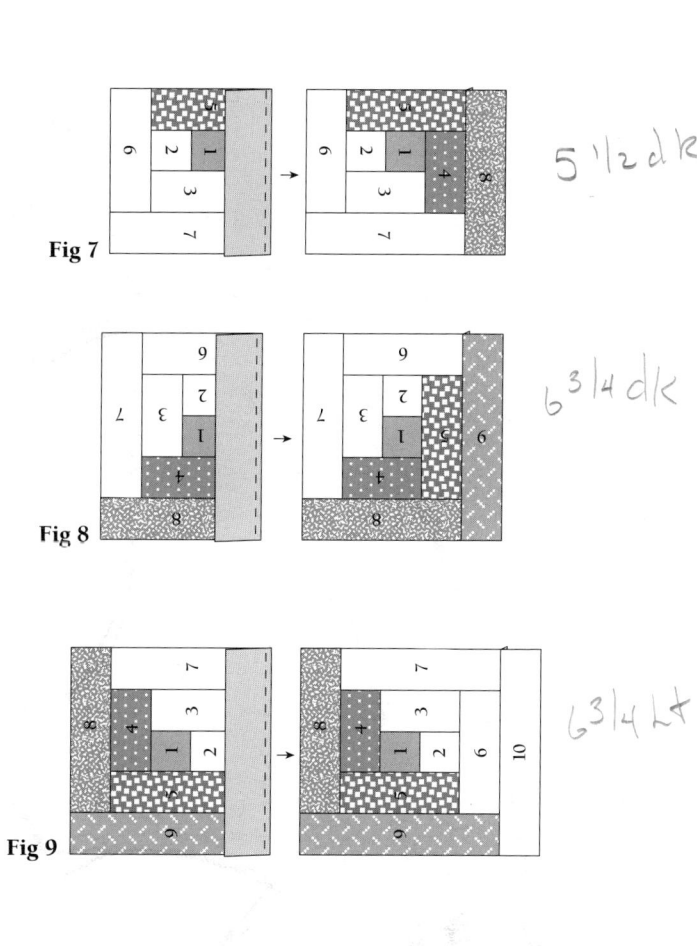

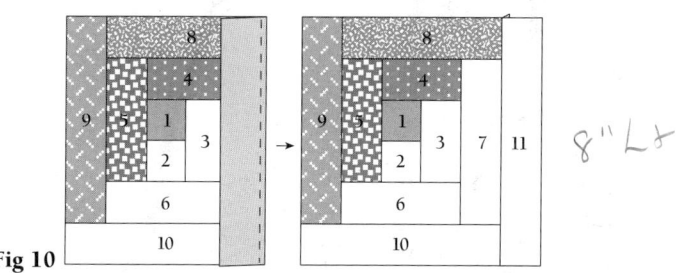

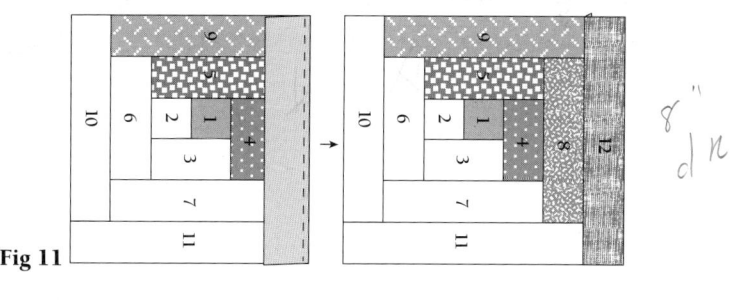

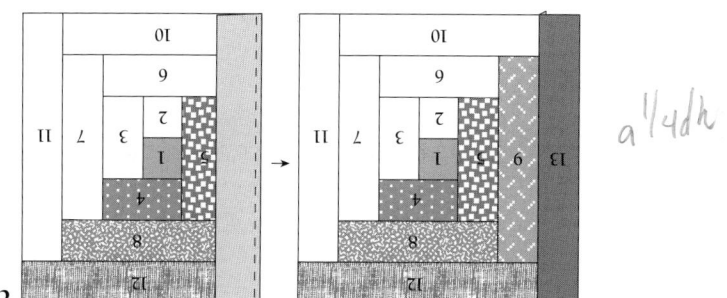

3. Repeat step 2 for 48 Log Cabin Blocks.

4. Sew four Log Cabin blocks together with light fabric strips toward center, **Fig 13**.

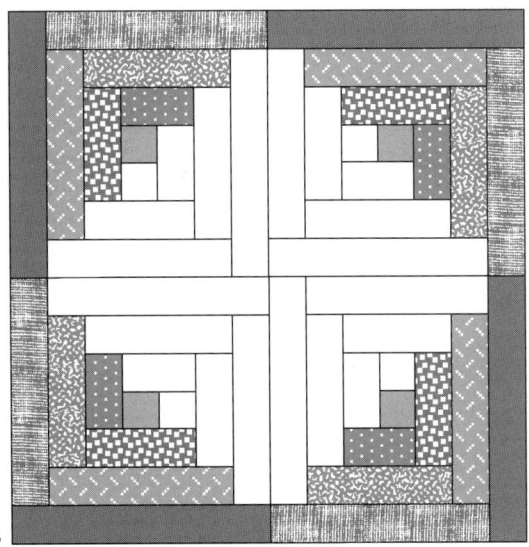

Fig 13

5. Repeat step 3 for a total of twelve Large Log Cabin blocks.

Appliquéd Flowers

1. Trace the following patterns onto paper side of fusible webbing:

- four A1 Flowers
- five A2 Flowers
- four B1 Flowers
- seven B2 Flowers
- eleven C Flowers
- eleven D Tulips
- 28 E Large Leaves
- 27 F Small Leaves
- five G Buds
- five H Calyx
- 31 I Flower Centers
- twelve J Baskets
- twelve K Basket Handles

2. Cut out each shape outside drawn line, **Fig 14**.

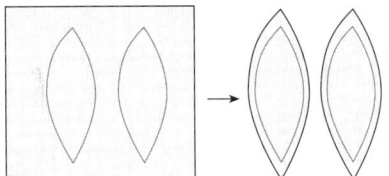

Fig 14

3. Press each shape onto the wrong side of selected fabric following manufacturer's instructions for fusible webbing.

4. Cut out along drawn line and remove paper backing.

5. Press fusible webbing onto wrong side of green stem fabric. Remove paper backing. Fold corner of strip down; press to crease. Cut along crease (which should be at a 45 degree angle), **Fig 15**. Continue cutting ½" strips using diagonal edge as a guide, **Fig 16**.

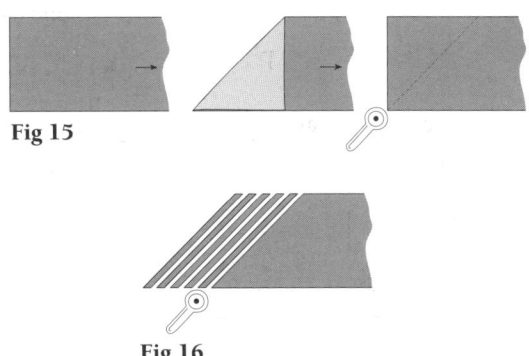

Fig 15

Fig 16

6. Referring to **Fig 17**, place baskets, flowers, leaves and stems (stems can be manipulated to curve in any direction) onto the light portion of the Large Log Cabin blocks.

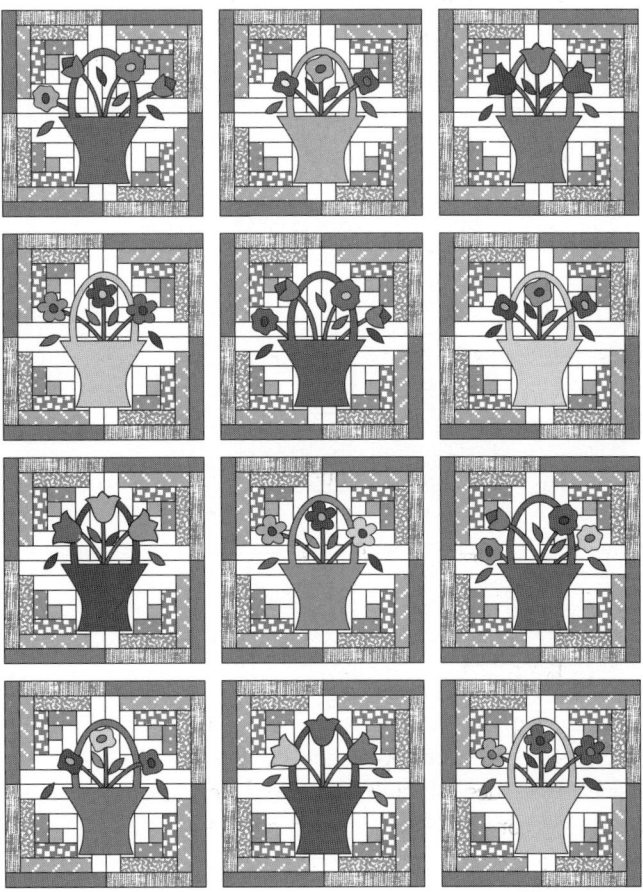

Fig 17

7. Press appliqué shapes in place following the instructions on the fusible webbing.

8. Following the instructions on page 5, Blanket stitch around all appliqué shapes.

Block Assembly and Borders

1. Lay out blocks referring to quilt layout on page 20. Sew blocks together in rows, then sew rows together.

2. Referring to **Fig 18** for placement, arrange Flowers, Stems and Leaves on the 8½" lt flannel corner squares, trimming stems as necessary.

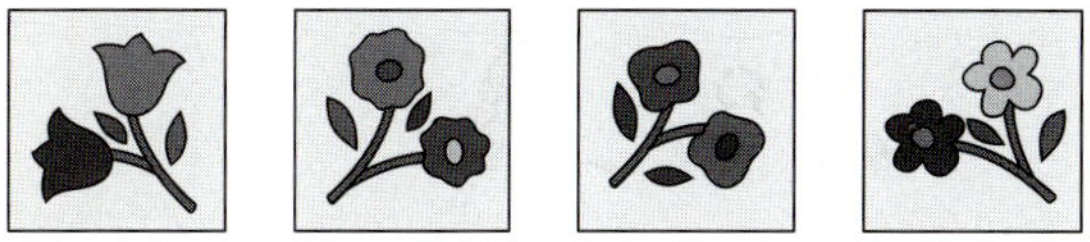

Fig 18

3. Work Blanket Stitch around all appliqué shapes.

4. For the first border, sew two 2" lt tan flannel strips together diagonally, **Fig 19**; press seam open. Repeat for remaining 2" border strips.

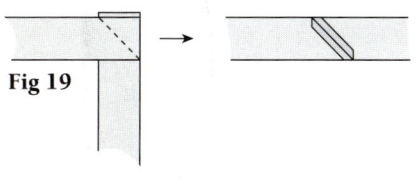

Fig 19

5. Measure length of quilt through middle. Cut two 2" border strips to that length. Sew a strip to each side of quilt.

6. Measure width of quilt through middle; cut remaining two border strips to that length. Sew strips to top and bottom of quilt.

7. For outside border, repeat step 4 for the 8½" dk flannel strips.

8. Measure quilt through the middle from side to side and from top to bottom. Sew borders to sides of quilt first. Sew an appliquéd corner square to each end of remaining border strips; sew to top and bottom of quilt.

Layering, Quilting and Binding

1. See pages 6 and 7 for layering and quilting. Photographed quilt was machine quilted around appliqué shapes. Chunky Stitch quilting, using the Quilting Pattern on page 25, was done around baskets and in both borders.

2. Using the Curve Outline, page 26, as a guide, draw scalloped edge around quilt; machine baste on drawn line.

3. Cut bias strips 2¼" wide for curved binding, then follow the Bias Binding instructions on page 8 to finish quilt.

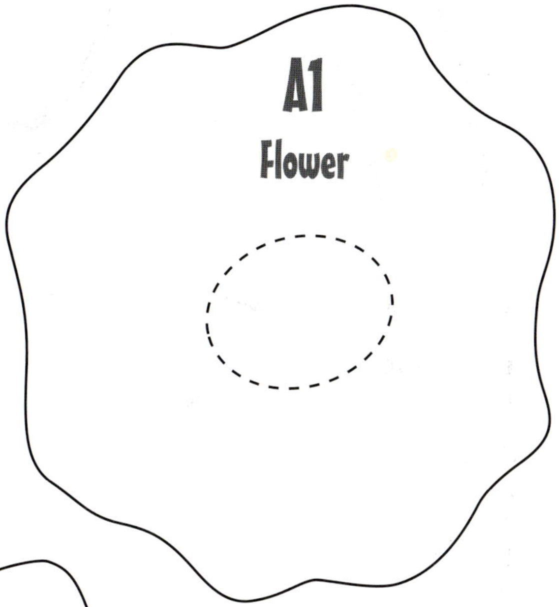

1 Flower Center

A1 Flower

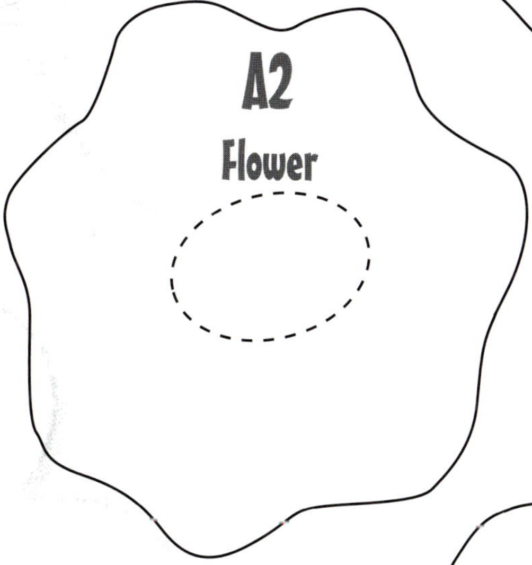

A2 Flower

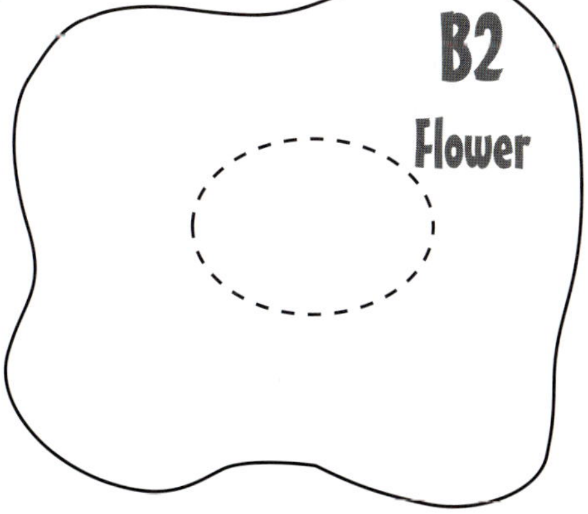

B2 Flower

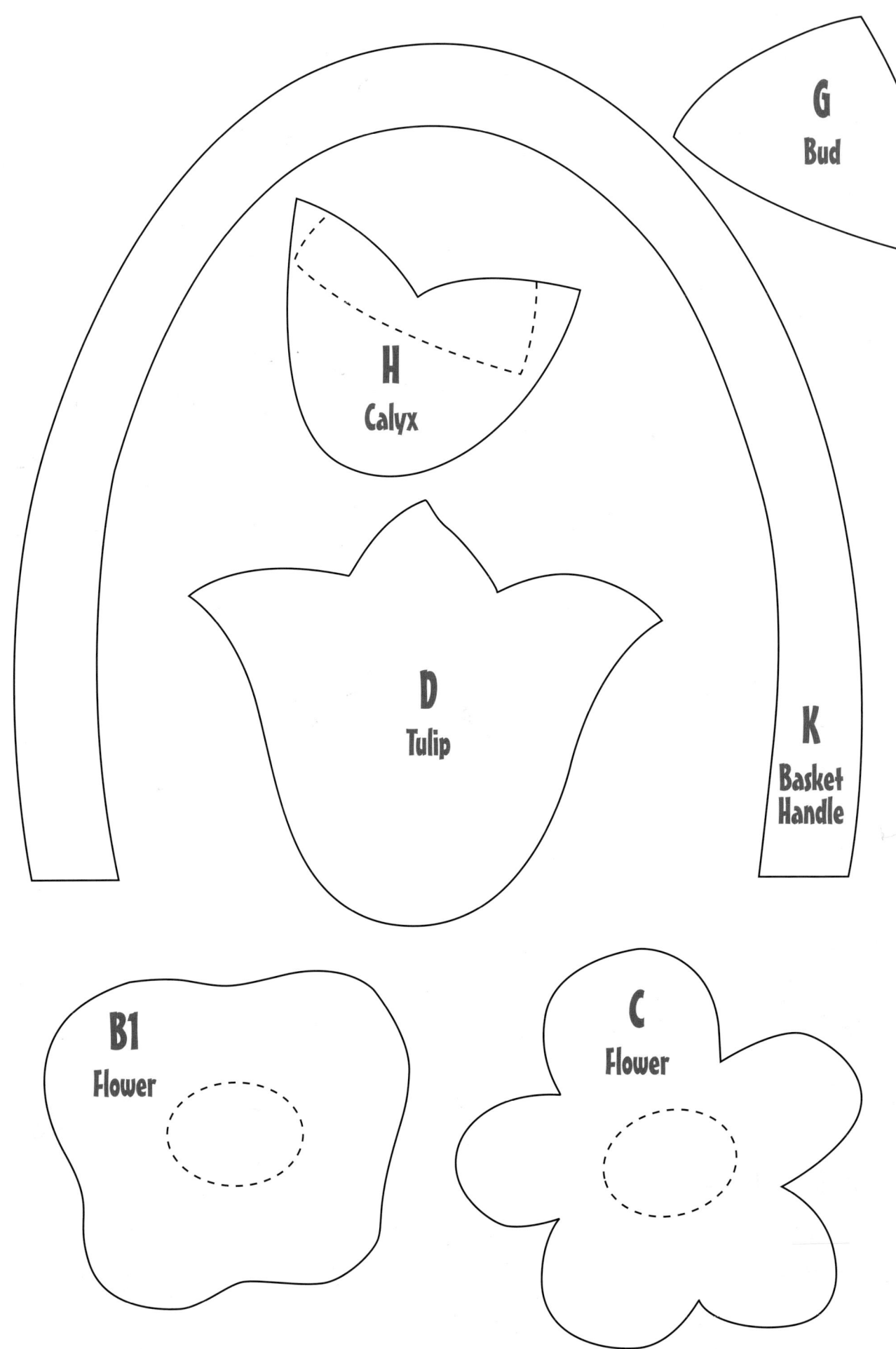

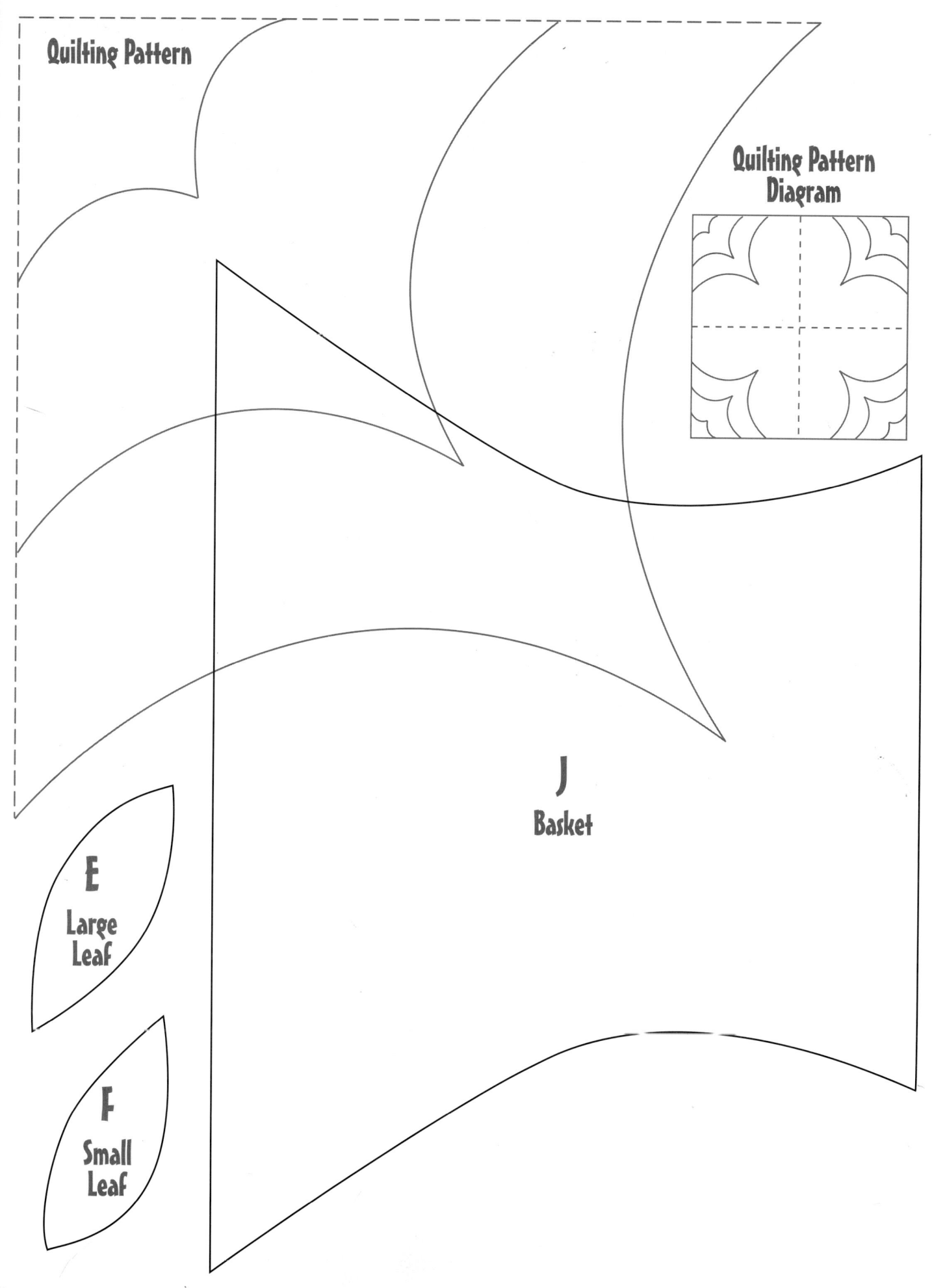

Corner Curve Guideline

Side Curve Guideline

My Soft Flannel Rose
by Krista Bateman

Lap Size Quilt Layout — *Shown in color photograph on page 13*

Approximate Lap Size: 59" x 73"
Approximate Bed Size: 74" x 87"

Snuggle up in a cozy flannel replica of the popular 1930's Ohio Rose pattern. Choose to make it either lap size or bed size. We give material amounts and instructions for both.

Materials and Supplies:
Note: Amounts are given for lap size with bed size in parentheses ( ).

3 (4 1/8) yds background flannel
1 (1 3/4) yds green print flannel (Leaves)
1 (1 3/4) yds solid red flannel (Large Petals & Buds)
1/2 (3/4) yd med blue flannel (Small Petals & Buds)
1/4 (1/4) yd dk blue flannel (Centers)
*2 (2 1/2) yds dk print flannel (inner border & binding)
2 1/2 (3) yds dk print flannel (outer border)
4 3/4 (6 3/4) yds backing
2 (2 3/4) yds 90"-wide lightweight batting
4 (6) yds 18"-wide fusible webbing
#5 pearl cotton for "Chunky Stitch Quilting"
embroidery needle

*A border print was used for the quilt model, but if unable to find a border print, substitute another fabric. The border was cut the length of the fabric rather than the width to eliminate seams.

Pattern Pieces (page 29):
A Center
B Large Petal
C Small Petal
D Leaf
E Bud

Cutting Requirements:
twelve (twenty) 14 1/2" squares*, background flannel
four 2" strips the length of the inner border fabric.**
four 2 1/2" strips the length of the inner border fabric for binding
four 8"-wide strips the length of the outer border fabric **

*These squares are cut oversized and will be squared to measure 14" after the applique is finished.

**These border strips are cut long enough to allow for mitering the corners.

Instructions:

Making the Flower Blocks
1. Trace each pattern piece the number of times as follows:

48 (80) Leaves
48 (80) Buds
48 (80) Large Petals
48 (80) Small Petals
12 (20) Centers

2. Fuse each traced section onto the wrong side of the selected fabric following manufacturer's instructions. After the fabric has cooled, cut out each shape. Remove paper backing.

3. Fold the background squares in half diagonally in both directions and lightly crease to create guidelines for placement of the flower pieces, **Fig 1**.

Fig 1

4. Referring to **Fig 2**, position the Center circle in middle of background square. Place four Large Petals so the inner edge is just barely under the Center circle. Add the Small Petals on top of Large Petals. Place Leaves on square next, tucking stem end slightly under Large Petal. Tuck Buds under the top edge of Leaves to complete block. Fuse in place following manufacturer's instructions.

Fig 2

5. Repeat step four for all twelve (twenty) blocks.

6. Work Blanket Stitch (see page 5) around each shape.

7. Press each block and trim to 14" square.

Assembling the Quilt.

1. Place blocks in four (five) rows of three (four) blocks. Sew together in rows, then sew rows together.

2. See pages 5 to 8 for adding the borders, mitering, layering, quilting and binding.

The photographed quilt was machine quilted around Flowers and Leaves and meander quilted in background of each block. Chunky Stitch quilting in a cable design was done in the large outer border.

Bed Size Quilt Layout